ALBUM II

10 Easy Pieces for Viola and Piano
from P. I. Tschaikowski, J. Brahms, M. I. Glinka, J. Ch. Wagenseil,
W. A. Mozart, F. Schubert, and C. M. von Weber

Edited by
Leonid Leibowitsch

DOWANI International

PREFACE

It is not always easy to find appropriate literature for beginners on the viola. With this edition (DOW 14502) and its predecessor (DOW 14501), we would like to offer you suitable literature in the form of easy pieces for novices.

The viola is very rarely studied as a first instrument, but often only after several years of lessons on the violin. We have therefore decided to include not only the "simple" keys (A, E, D, G) and finger positions, but also relatively easy pieces in the more unusual keys of C, F and B-flat. Our editor, Leonid Leibowitsch, has been very judicious in his selection of pieces.

Concerning the musical text, the pieces are relatively easy to play. This enables you to concentrate fully on the music, to hear and grasp it consciously and to take a more active part in the musical interpretation. *DOWANI 3 Tempi Play Along* offers you an ideal starting point for this.

We have deliberately refrained from including fingerings in the solo voice. This allows every teacher to work out the fingerings appropriate to the pupil and to mark them down on the page. You will also find fingering suggestions from Leonid Leibowitsch in the piano part – for the piano as well as for the viola.

Each selection on our CD begins with the concert version. After tuning your instrument (Track 1), the musical work can begin. Your first practice session should be in the slow tempo. If your stereo system is equipped with a balance control, you can, by turning the control, smoothly blend either the viola or the piano accompaniment into the foreground. The viola, however, will always remains audible – even if very quietly – as a guide. In the middle position, both instruments can be heard at the same volume. If you do not have a balance control, you can listen to the solo instrument on one loudspeaker and to the piano on the other. After you have studied the selection in the slow tempo, you can advance to the intermediate and original tempi. The piano can be heard at these tempi on both channels (without viola) in stereo quality. All of the pieces were recorded live. The names of the musicians are listed on the last page of this volume; further information can be found in the Internet at www.dowani.com.

We wish you lots of fun playing from our *DOWANI 3 Tempi Play Along* editions and hope that your musicality and diligence will enable you to play the concert version as soon as possible.

It is our goal to give you the essential conditions for effective practicing through motivation, enjoyment and fun.

Your DOWANI-Team

AVANT-PROPOS

Il n'est pas toujours facile de trouver des morceaux d'alto pour débutants. Avec ce recueil (DOW 14502) et le recueil précédent (DOW 14501), nous vous proposons un répertoire facile qui convient aux débutants.

Nous avons décidé de ne pas choisir seulement des morceaux dans les tonalités "faciles" (La, Mi, Ré, Sol) et dans des positions faciles, car il est plutôt rare que l'on apprend l'alto comme premier instrument. C'est pourquoi vous trouverez également des morceaux faciles dans des tonalités inhabituelles au début (Do, Fa et Si bémol). Notre rédacteur, Leonid Leibowitsch, a préparé une sélection judicieuse.

En ce qui concerne le texte musical, le degré de difficulté des morceaux choisis se situe dans la catégorie "facile". Vous pourrez ainsi vous concentrer entièrement sur la musique, bien l'écouter et la comprendre et, ensuite, vous investir activement dans son interprétation. La collection "DOWANI 3 Tempi Play Along" constitue pour cela un point de départ idéal.

Nous avons délibérément renoncé à indiquer des doigtés dans la partie soliste. Chaque professeur a ainsi la possibilité d'élaborer avec l'élève des doigtés appropriés et de les noter dans la partition. De plus, vous trouverez dans la partition de l'accompagnement de piano des suggestions par Leonid Leibowitsch concernant les doigtés, non seulement pour le piano, mais aussi pour l'alto.

Le CD vous permettra d'entendre d'abord la version de concert de chaque morceau. Après avoir accordé votre instrument (plage N° 1), vous pouvez commencer le travail musical. Votre premier contact avec le morceau devrait se faire à un tempo lent. Si votre chaîne hi-fi dispose d'un réglage de balance, vous pouvez l'utiliser pour mettre au premier plan soit l'alto, soit l'accompagnement de piano. L'alto restera cependant toujours très doucement à l'arrière-plan comme point de repère. En équilibrant la balance, vous entendrez les deux instruments à volume égal. Si vous ne disposez pas de réglage de balance, vous entendrez l'instrument soliste sur un des haut-parleurs et le piano sur l'autre. Après avoir étudié le morceau à un tempo lent, vous pourrez ensuite travailler à un tempo modéré et au tempo original. Dans ces deux tempos vous entendrez l'accompagnement de piano sur les deux canaux en stéréo (sans la partie d'alto). Toutes les œuvres ont été enregistrées en direct. Vous trouverez les noms des artistes qui ont participé aux enregistrements sur la dernière page de cette édition ; pour obtenir plus de renseignements, veuillez consulter notre site Internet : www.dowani.com.

Nous vous souhaitons beaucoup de plaisir à faire de la musique avec la collection "DOWANI 3 Tempi Play Along" et nous espérons que votre musicalité et votre application vous amèneront aussi rapidement que possible à la version de concert.

Notre but est de vous offrir les bases nécessaires pour un travail efficace par la motivation et le plaisir.

Les Éditions DOWANI

VORWORT

Nicht immer ist es leicht, entsprechende Anfänger-literatur für Viola zu finden. Mit dieser Ausgabe (DOW 14502) und der vorherigen (DOW 14501) wollen wir Ihnen in Form von leichten Stücken passende Literatur für den Anfängerbereich bieten.

Da Viola sehr selten als Erstinstrument erlernt wird, sondern oft erst nach einigen Jahren des Violinunterrichts, haben wir uns entschieden, nicht nur die „einfachen" Tonarten (A, E, D, G) und Griffe aufzunehmen, sondern auch leichtere Stücke in den nicht gleich üblichen Tonarten C, F und B. Die Auswahl der Stücke ist unserem Herausgeber, Leonid Leibowitsch, sehr gut gelungen.

Was den Notentext betrifft, so liegt der Schwie-rigkeitsgrad der Stücke im leichteren Bereich. Da-durch können Sie sich ganz auf die Musik kon-zentrieren, sie bewusst hören und verstehen und sich infolgedessen selbst aktiv in die musikalische Interpretation einbringen. Dafür bietet Ihnen *DOWANI 3 Tempi Play Along* eine optimale Ausgangsbasis.

Wir haben bewusst auf alle Fingersätze in der Solo-Stimme verzichtet. Jeder Pädagoge hat somit die Möglichkeit, mit dem Schüler zusammen die für ihn passenden Fingersätze zu erarbeiten und im Notentext zu notieren. Darüber hinaus finden Sie als Anregung in der Klavierstimme Fingersatz-Vorschläge von Leonid Leibowitsch – sowohl für Klavier als auch für Viola.

Auf der CD hören Sie zuerst die Konzertversion eines jeden Stückes. Nach dem Stimmen Ihres Instrumentes (Track 1) kann die musikalische Arbeit beginnen. Ihr erster Übe-Kontakt mit dem Stück sollte im langsamen Tempo stattfinden. Wenn Ihre Stereoanlage über einen Balance-Regler verfügt, können Sie durch Drehen des Reglers entweder nur die Viola oder die Klavierbegleitung stufenlos in den Vordergrund blenden. Die Viola bleibt jedoch immer als Orientierungshilfe – wenn auch sehr leise – hörbar. In der Mittelposition erklingen beide Instrumente gleich laut. Falls Sie keinen Balance-Regler haben, hören Sie das Soloinstrument auf einem Lautsprecher, das Kla-vier auf dem anderen. Nachdem Sie das Stück im langsamen Tempo einstudiert haben, können Sie danach im mittelschnellen und originalen Tempo musizieren. Das Klavier erklingt hierbei auf beiden Kanälen (ohne Viola) in Stereo-Qualität. Alle Werke wurden live aufgenommen. Die Namen der Künstler finden Sie auf der letzten Seite dieser Ausgabe; ausführlichere Informationen können Sie im Internet unter www.dowani.com nachlesen.

Wir wünschen Ihnen viel Spaß beim Musizieren aus *DOWANI 3 Tempi Play Along*-Ausgaben und hoffen, dass Ihre Musikalität und Ihr Fleiß Sie möglichst bald bis zur Konzertversion führen werden.

Unser Ziel ist es, Ihnen durch Motivation und Freude die notwendigen Voraussetzungen für effektives Üben zu schaffen.

Ihr DOWANI Team

I

Elderberry on the Field

Traditional (Russia)
Arrangement: P. I. Tschaikowski

DOW 14502

II

The Crane

Traditional (Ukraine)
Arrangement: P. I. Tschaikowski

III

Jumping Jack

J. Brahms (1833 – 1897)

IV

The little Nightingale

M. Glinka (1804 – 1857)

ALBUM II

10 Easy Pieces for Viola and Piano
from P. I. Tschaikowski, J. Brahms, M. I. Glinka, J. Ch. Wagenseil,
W. A. Mozart, F. Schubert, and C. M. von Weber

Viola / Alto / Viola

DOWANI International

Viola

I ②

Elderberry on the Field

Traditional (Russia)
Arrangement: P. I. Tschaikowski

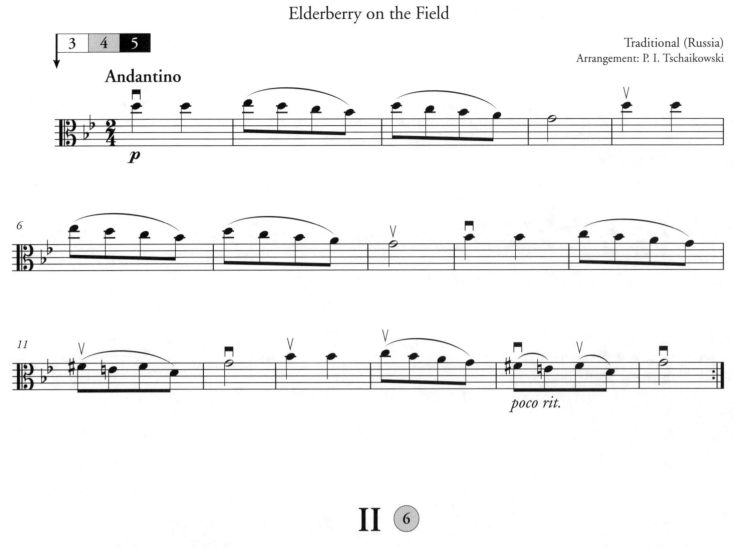

II ⑥

The Crane

Traditional (Ukraine)
Arrangement: P. I. Tschaikowski

DOW 14502

III ⑩

Jumping Jack

J. Brahms (1833 – 1897)

IV ⑭

The little Nightingale

M. Glinka (1804 – 1857)

V ⓲

To make Hay

Traditional (Russia)
Arrangement: P. I. Tschaikowski

VI ㉒

Valse

W. A. Mozart (1756 – 1791)

VII

Minuet

J. Ch. Wagenseil (1715 – 1779)

VIII 30

Minuet

W. A. Mozart (1756 – 1791)

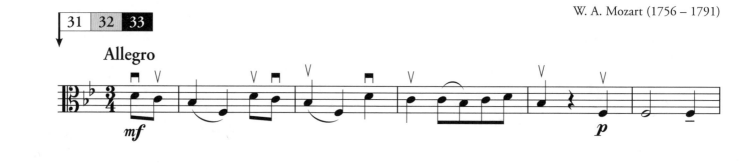

DOW 14502

IX

Valse

F. Schubert (1797 – 1828)

X 38

Valse

C. M. von Weber (1786 – 1826)

V

To make Hay

Traditional (Russia)
Arrangement: P. I. Tschaikowski

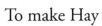
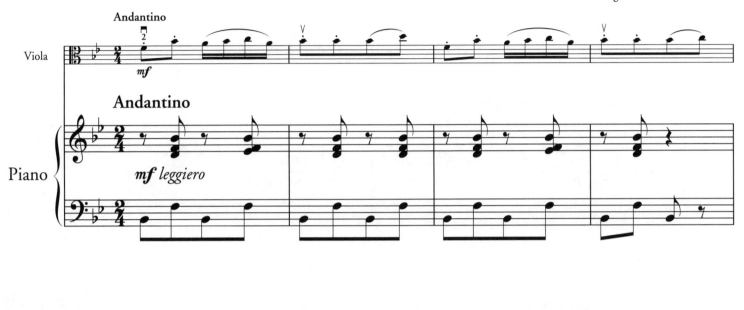

VI

Valse

W. A. Mozart (1756 – 1791)

VII

Minuet

J. Ch. Wagenseil (1715 – 1779)

DOW 14502

VIII

Minuet

W. A. Mozart (1756 – 1791)

IX

Valse

F. Schubert (1797 – 1828)

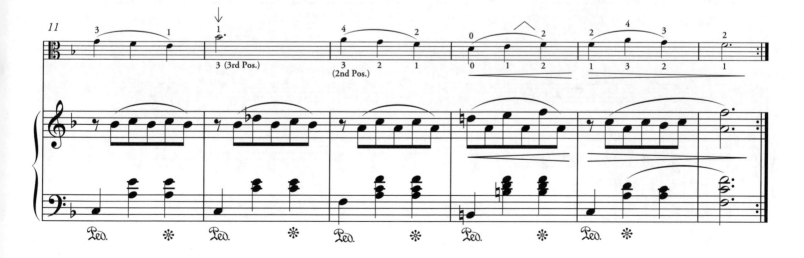

X

Valse

C. M. von Weber (1786 – 1826)

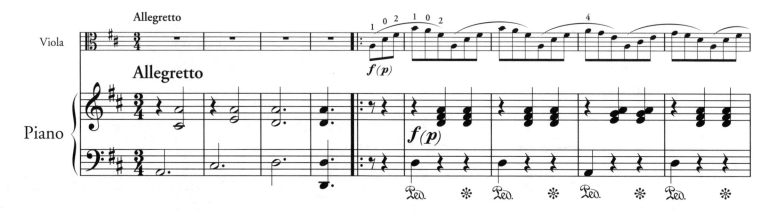

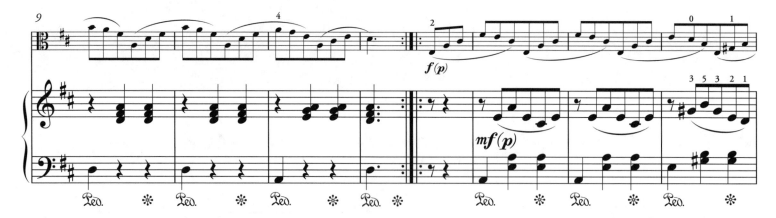

ENGLISH

DOWANI CD:
- Track nr. 1
- Track numbers in circles
- Track numbers in squares

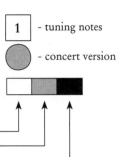

- tuning notes
- concert version

- slow Play Along Tempo
- intermediate Play Along Tempo
- original Play Along Tempo

- **Concert version:** viola and piano

- **Slow tempo:** the viola can be faded in or out by means of the balance control, Channel 1: viola solo, Channel 2: piano accompaniment with viola in the background, Middle position: both channels at the same volume

- **Intermediate tempo:** piano accompaniment only

- **Original tempo:** piano accompaniment only

FRANÇAIS

DOWANI CD:
- Plage N° 1
- N° de plage dans un cercle
- N° de plage dans un rectangle

- diapason
- version de concert

- Tempo lent play along
- Tempo moyen play along
- Tempo original play along

- **Version de concert :** alto et piano

- **Tempo lent :** Vous pouvez choisir – en réglant la balance du lecteur CD – entre les versions avec ou sans alto.
  1er canal : alto solo ; 2nd canal : accompagnement de piano avec alto en fond sonore ; au milieu : les deux canaux au même volume.

- **Tempo moyen :** seulement l'accompagnement de piano.

- **Tempo original :** seulement l'accompagnement de piano.

DEUTSCH

DOWANI CD:
- Track Nr. 1
- Trackangabe im Kreis
- Trackangabe im Rechteck

- Stimmtöne
- Konzertversion

- langsames Play Along Tempo
- mittleres Play Along Tempo
- originales Play Along Tempo

- **Konzertversion:** Viola und Klavier

- **Langsames Tempo:** Ein- und ausblenden der Viola mittels Balance-Regler, 1. Kanal: Viola solo, 2. Kanal: Klavierbegleitung mit Viola im Hintergrund, Mitte: Beide Kanäle in gleicher Lautstärke.

- **Mittleres Tempo:** nur Klavierbegleitung

- **Originaltempo:** nur Klavierbegleitung

DOWANI - 3 Tempi Play Along is published by:
DOWANI International Est.
Industriestrasse 24 / Postfach 156, FL-9487 Bendern,
Principality of Liechtenstein
Phone: ++423 370 11 15, Fax ++423 370 19 44
E-Mail: info@dowani.com
www.dowani.com

Digital Mastering: Pavel Lavrenenkov, Russia
CD-Production: Sonopress, Germany
Music notation by Notensatz Thomas Metzinger, Germany
Design: Atelier Schuster, Austria
Printed by Buchdruckerei Lustenau, Austria
Made in the Principality of Liechtenstein

Concert Version
Alexander Akimov, Viola
Vitaly Junitsky, Piano

3 Tempi Accompaniment
Slow:
Vitaly Junitsky, Piano

Intermediate:
Vitaly Junitsky, Piano

Original:
Vitaly Junitsky, Piano